Bridget K. Lambright

Middle School to the Max!

School Shouldn't Be Pointless

Bridget Lambright-Tommelleo, M.Ed.

(Middle School to the Max!)

Copyright © 2023 by Bridget K. Lambright

All rights reserved. No part of this publication may be reproduced, distributed, or transmitted in any form or by any means, including photocopying, recording, or other electronic or mechanical methods, without the prior written permission of the publisher, except in the case of brief quotations embodied in critical reviews and certain other noncommercial uses permitted by copyright law. For permission requests, email the publisher, at maximizeschool@gmail.com.

www.maximizeschool.com

Ordering Information:

Quantity sales. Special discounts are available on quantity purchases by schools, corporations, associations, and others. For details, contact the publisher at the website above.

Printed in the United States of America

ISBN 978-0-9796578-4-9

Bridget K. Lambright

Gal, don't be common.

- V. Melvin-Lambright aka Aunt Vi

Middle School to the Max!

Bridget K. Lambright

Acknowledgements

For the hundredth time, I didn't choose teaching. Teaching chose me. And boy, am I glad it did. It's been an incredible journey. I've met some of the most inspirational and impressive individuals on earth — my students. I am forever indebted to them for helping me become the best version of myself. It's been a daily blessing to witness their growth (both in and out of the classroom).

To my former students, I apologize for being a bit fanatical about preparing you for life after high school. Please understand that it's only because I want you to succeed. Watching you all achieve your goals and dreams has been the most fulfilling experience of my career.

And to Ms. Arnetha, with her beautiful big afro, amazing smile, loving laugh, and dashiki. I can't thank you enough. You were my preschool teacher. Every day you made me feel smart, pretty, and special. You laid the foundation for my future success. I am eternally grateful.

I must also give a special shout-out to my French teacher at Bella Vista High School. Madame has been my only K-12 teacher that I have ever been able to remember. Her ability to make me feel like a rockstar on a daily basis was second to none. She brought her unique teaching style all the way from Paris, France to Fair Oaks, California. This was a game-changer for me. She'll never know how much she helped me survive some very difficult days.

Finally, to my little family, who taught me the true power of love. I didn't understand this feeling until I birthed my children and married my husband. They inspire me to be better every day. I'm breaking generational curses because of them. Their love motivates me to give more than I ever thought was possible.

Ms. BLT

Bridget K. Lambright

Contents

Acknowledgements	5
Contents	7
Introduction	8
Self-Monitoring Tool for The High School Ready Student	16
Be Analytical	27
Be Creative	32
Be a Problem – Solver	38
Be a Visionary	44
Be Prepared	51
Be Impressive	57
Be Prompt	65
Be an Active Listener	73
Be a Writer	79
Be Cooperative	91
Be Engaged	107
Be Steady	114

Middle School to the Max!

Introduction

Hello there!

I'm thrilled that you've decided to join me on this mission. It looks like someone in your life (maybe your teacher, school district, or parent) believes that this resource can benefit you. I couldn't agree more.

Before we dive in, let me give you fair warning: this manual isn't going to sugarcoat **anything**. I'm not here to talk down to you or treat you like a baby. You're capable of handling the truth. That's exactly what I'm going to give you. Trust me, I know that being talked down to is annoying and disrespectful. So, let's get real. Now is a good time to talk about what it takes to be successful.

As for me, I've had the privilege of helping over 2,000 students graduate from high school and excel in life. I don't plan on stopping anytime soon. But, I do have a huge confession to make.

I. Couldn't. Help. Everybody.

As much as it pains me to say it, not all of those 2,000 students were eager to listen to my advice. Some weren't ready for the truth. Others simply didn't care about their future. For some, the idea of graduating from high school seemed impossible — especially if they didn't have any family members who had done it before. I'll admit, there were even a few students who were negative all the time. They rejected every warning that I tried to share. My heart still hurts *every time* I have to say this to people.

Here are four **real facts** about high school dropouts*:

1) Every year, over 1.2 million students drop out of high school in the United States alone. That's a student every 26 seconds or 7,000 a day.

2) A high school dropout will earn $200,000 less than a high school graduate over his/her lifetime. And almost a million dollars less than a college graduate.

3) In the United States, high school dropouts commit about 75% of crimes.

4) High school dropouts are more susceptible to lifestyle problems:
    - 56.8% of high school dropouts smoke cigarettes
    - 41.6% of high school dropouts drink alcohol
    - 32.3% of high school dropouts binge alcohol
    - 31.4% of high school dropouts use an illicit drug

Middle School to the Max!

- 27.3% of high school dropouts use marijuana

Hmmm, maybe someone cares about you so much that he/she wants to make sure that you never become one of these statistics. I want to help you because you're too young to understand how crazy hard your adult life can be depending on your choices. As an educator, I've seen far too many high school dropouts struggle to make ends meet. They can't  afford nutritious meals. They can't afford to move to safer neighborhoods. They can't even afford to take care of their own health. I've even witnessed parents pass away while leaving their adult children without any money to give them a proper burial. It's tough to see people suffer like that. Especially when they're suffering from pain that they created for themselves starting in middle school. I hope you know that you don't have to be one of those statistics.

It's completely up to you to decide. Are you already taking charge of your education and your future? With the tips and advice in this manual, you'll have everything you need to graduate from high school and succeed in life. And let me tell you, this isn't just another empty promise. I've had hundreds of former students use my advice. They went on to become incredibly successful adults. It's amazing to hear their stories about how they were able to apply what they learned. Now, they're living better lives than they ever thought possible. Knowledge is power when you use it to do something beneficial. If you don't act, all that knowledge will just make you bitter. Deep down inside, you'll have regrets (woulda-coulda-shoulda) and wish that you had made better choices.

Do you know that every year thousands of middle school students go to high school, but they flunk, drop out, or get expelled?

It's a hard pill to swallow, but America has millions of high school dropouts. Even more concerning, there are millions of people in this country who lack basic reading and math skills. More than half of the adults in America read below a sixth grader. Their deficits are making it nearly impossible for them to find a job that pays a livable wage with benefits. The sad reality is that many of these individuals were led to believe that they could breeze through high school without putting in the effort. Those with low reading comprehension and writing skills just kept falling further behind.

Middle School to the Max!

High school isn't middle school. It's a whole different vibe. The work is harder. The expectations are higher. The consequences for falling behind are **much** more severe. Picture stubbing your toe in the middle of the night versus slamming a car door on your fingers. Plus, the automatic door lock traps your smashed hand! High school is about preparing you for the real world. A world where you can't just coast by and expect everything to be *handed* to you.

That's why I created this manual — not to scare you, but to prepare you. I want you to understand that your attitude, behavior, work ethic, and intelligence will all play a critical role in your high school experience. **I'm just here to tell you that your high school teachers expect you to commit your best and be your best version of yourself.**

There are bad behaviors that a student can have in elementary and middle school that will make him/her earn pathetic grades, miss out on activities or clubs, lose adults' respect, fail a high school class, or even get kicked out of high school. This is how a kid gets lumped into those bad statistics I mentioned earlier. Yes, high school students can get sent home permanently. Am I describing you? If you don't fix those bad behaviors right now, they'll become bad habits. If you're already maximizing your time in middle school, those good behaviors will become good habits. Habits are very hard to unlearn. If you keep on demonstrating high school readiness, then you'll truly be prepared for when it's finally time to graduate from high school.

Middle school is not the place to be a slacker. Your willingness to get ready for high school right now will determine whether you'll be a high school graduate, flunky, or dropout. I've met many students who said they would be doctors, accountants, lawyers, scientists, athletes, teachers, engineers, or business owners, but their bad habits kept them from learning and growing. Instead of putting all their energy into catching up or getting ahead, they played around and kept sliding backwards. Their focused classmates kept moving ahead without them. Congratulations to the students who are headed in the right direction! Grownups don't say it enough, but having students who come to school to learn is THE BEST! Sadly, students who never make their futures a priority **before** high school will struggle the most **in** high school.

Graduating from high school *with* a 2.8 GPA (grade point average) *or above* will probably be one of the hardest challenges you'll face as a kid. Maintaining excellent attendance and a high grade point average are as important as drinking water. The more (higher), the better. Your graduation with a good-to-great GPA will also be one of the best moves you'll ever make before you become an adult. I don't want to scare you because high school should be fun too. You'll have interesting classes, friends, parties, clubs, games, events, and opportunities. It's a completely different world from what you're seeing, hearing, and feeling right now. **After you're a high school graduate, your fun experiences can get even bigger and better!** So, please keep reading this book to discover more about what school has to offer. There are tasks in this manual to help you get the most from all this information. Don't worry, students before you have said that the activities are easy and they help with remembering the topics. Now, let's dive into getting you ready for high school and your dream life.

Bridget K. Lambright

I really enjoyed the manual and I feel motivated to improve my performance in high school. I plan on using these next two years to get my grades up and be more involved in my education.

— Daniel, HS Student

Even though I'm barely passing the class, I feel if I got a second chance to do it again I would achieve. Although I should have used and activated my high school readiness skills in every class. The book was very good and will be a great source for the rest of middle school.

— Jameer, MS Student

This helped me out a lot and to find out what I need to change in my life for high school and college.

— Ashley, HS Student

Ms. Lambright really taught me a lot about self-discipline and time management (which is very important in college). If you want to reduce some of the anxiety related to the first day, week, month or year of college (school) then read the book and apply the tips!

— Rhonnetta, BSW & MSW from The Ohio State University

*https://www.dosomething.org/us/facts/11-facts-about-high-school-dropout-rates

(Middle School to the Max!)

Self-Monitoring Tool for The High School Ready Student

This self-assessment was created for you. The purpose of completing this survey is to increase your awareness about what high school teachers will expect. You're not in high school yet, so you really don't know what you don't know. This survey will help you pinpoint specific areas that may need your attention. Every single day, your classes give you a chance to develop into an outstanding high school graduate and successful adult in the future.

Please be completely honest with yourself.

	Description Statements (Mark "X" in each column that best describes you, your attitude, and your conduct)	Not at all	Not enough	Some what	Most of the time	All the time
	My Brain					
1.	I am analytical and creative, so I avoid stating the obvious or borrowing ideas that have already been presented in class.					
2.	I explore and attempt resourceful ways to solve challenges instead of					

		Not at all	Not enough	Some what	Most of the time	All the time
	getting frustrated and giving up.					
3.	I make positive choices to protect my future.					
	Description Statements (Mark "X" in each column that best describes you, your attitude, and your conduct)	Not at all	Not enough	Some what	Most of the time	All the time
	My Assignments					
4.	I come to class with all my books, papers, pencils, and required supplies without having to borrow or retrieve missing items.					
5.	My homework is labeled correctly and completely ready BEFORE school starts.					
6.	I take pride in my work by making sure that it is 100% complete, neat, clean, wrinkle-free, original, amazing, proof-read, and error-free.					
7.	I meet every deadline without using hall passes, tardiness, or absences to get more time.					

Middle School to the Max!

	My Mouth, Eyes, Ears, Hands, and Feet					
8.	I never complain, blame, or make excuses.					
9.	I spend more time reading and writing than getting on social media, watching television, and playing with my devices.					
	Description Statements (Mark "X" in each column that best describes you, your attitude, and your conduct)	Not at all	Not enough	Some what	Most of the time	All the time
10.	I am never defiant, disruptive, or a distraction.					
11.	I contribute to learning by sitting up, staying focused, listening closely, making relevant comments, and asking useful questions.					
	My Heart					
12.	I display a positive attitude and maintain my					

	composure regardless of what is said or done to me.					
13.	I am a considerate person who works well with different personalities in the classroom.					
14.	I am flexible and comply whenever the teacher or a guest announces directions, activities, due dates, etc.					
15.	I am a motivated, hard worker in every class.					

My Overall Mindset

16.	I arrive before class starts, set-up promptly, and am ready for the day's activities or lessons without needing to be told.					
	Description Statements (Mark "X" in each column that best describes you, your attitude, and your conduct)	Not at all	Not enough	Some what	Most of the time	All the time
17.	I follow the school's rules for attendance, dress code, devices, conflict resolution, bad language, etc.					
18.	I strive to be impressive and a top scholar.					

19.	I am constantly focused on mastering the knowledge, skills, and abilities to graduate from high school, earn a certification, graduate from college, and earn livable wages ($35+ an hour) with benefits.					

Bridget K. Lambright

	Scoring	Not at all	Not enough	Some what	Most of the time	All the time
Step 1	Add the number of check marks for each column and write the total for each column under the matching heading in the boxes.					
Step 2	Multiply the total for each column by the red number in the box and write the answer for that column after the equal sign.	x1 =	x1 =	x2 =	x3 =	x4 =
Step 3	Add all of your answers together in Step #2 for your overall High School Readiness score.					

Thank you for taking this survey seriously. When you go to the doctor, he/she cannot help you get healthy or stay healthy without assessing your status. That's why your honest answers were so important. Yes, #10 is stated in the negative. Please make sure that your response is correct. If you had some thoughts and questions while taking this survey, that's good. But wait, there's more. Please take a minute to check your final calculations one more time before the last step.

Middle School to the Max!

Here's what your final answer reveals about how you're doing with maximizing your middle school experience:

76 - 68 = High School Ready
67 - 61 = Mostly High School Ready
60 - 53 = Somewhat High School Ready
52 - 46 = Limited High School Readiness
45 - ⇩ = Barely High School Ready

One key to success in high school and beyond is scoring high on your quizzes, tests, and exams. If you're not happy with these scores, it's time to ask yourself some tough questions. How badly do you want your dreams to come true? Is having a successful adult life important to you? Are you hungry? The good news is that there's still plenty of time to make the most of your middle school and high school years.

This survey is over twenty years old, but the numbers don't lie. When students are completely honest, they're able to see where they stand and what they need to work on. Think of it like a  doctor's appointment. Sometimes patients get angry at their test results, but they can't get better without knowing their actual numbers. This survey was created to help you like it has helped hundreds of students before you. And even if your scores turned out great, there's always room for improvement. Perfect students don't exist. Everyone, especially adults, can benefit from constantly working to be a better version of themselves.

(Middle School to the Max!)

High School Readiness Task

Before you start reading tips in this manual, please write down 3-5 areas that have the lowest scores on your high school readiness survey:

1) _____
_____

2) _____
_____

3) _____
_____

4) _____
_____

Now, have your teacher or parent identify an area that he/she thinks you should pay close attention to:

5) _____
_____

*While you're reading the rest of this manual, please **pay EXTRA attention to:**

- *The areas that you listed.*
- *Brainstorming ways to improve.*
- *Getting support from your teachers.*
- *Committing yourself to preparing for your high school graduation every day.*

Middle School to the Max!

High School Readiness Task

At the end of every topic, this section is for you to write down 3-5 important ideas that your future high school self will need your middle school self to remember.

_____
_____
_____
_____
_____
_____
_____
_____
_____

Bridget K. Lambright

Be Analytical

You've probably heard the story about Goldilocks, Mama Bear, Papa Bear, and Baby Bear. If you're not familiar with it, a quick Google search will fill you in. Now imagine your teacher asks the class to analyze Goldilocks' character. If someone simply answers that she's a girl, your teacher is likely thinking, "Duh!" The truth is, that answer isn't analytical at all — it's stating the obvious. When you're analyzing a character or any other subject, you need to dig deeper and look for greater meaning. To truly analyze a character, you need to provide an answer that others may not see. You may even have to debate to prove your point.

The answer is not in the text, it's in your noggin (brain). It comes from your personality, experiences, and wisdom. You're one of a kind and so is your analytical response.

Honestly, you're doing nothing more than making your brain lazy when all you do is state what's obvious. The brain is a muscle. The more you exercise this muscle by figuring out meanings and making predictions, the stronger it gets. Without muscles, our bodies would be limp like wet noodles. You need your muscles to walk and lift your arms. High school is harder and expects more from you. You're going to need your brain to be in great shape. The stronger, the better. I've visited middle schools where students deliberately clogged toilets without any thought of the consequences. In response to the vandalism, their teachers and principals took away their privileges and treated them like younger elementary students. Duh, baby behavior (reckless) deserves baby treatment (restrictions). These kids haven't figured out yet how **every** action has a reaction.

Now is the time to start exercising your brain every day with analysis. Practice truly does make perfect. The more you challenge yourself to think critically, the better you'll become. So, please take a chance during class and don't be afraid to speak up. Your teachers are there to help you improve each day.

Remember, when you're analyzing something, it's important to leave the obvious where it belongs — in the text. Instead, try to dig deeper and make connections that others might not see. The more analytical you are, the more you'll impress your teachers and classmates. Analytical students make awesome high school graduates. Guess what, the more you know and the better you are at critical thinking, the more future jobs **will** pay you.

Middle School to the Max!

Reflecting on Your High School Readiness

1) How would your life be better if you were more **analytical** (don't just repeat the text)?

_____
_____
_____
_____

2) What do you need to do to be more **analytical** (you know yourself best, so dig deep and keep it real with yourself)?

_____
_____
_____
_____

3) What was your *aha* moment while reading about this topic?

_____
_____
_____
_____

Bridget K. Lambright

High School Readiness Task

At the end of every topic, this section is for you to write down 3-5 important ideas that your future high school self will need your middle school self to remember.

_____
_____
_____
_____
_____
_____
_____
_____
_____
_____

Middle School to the Max!

Be Creative

When you meet new people, you immediately judge whether or not you'll like them based on how they look, behave, and what they say. These same people are probably using the same criteria to judge whether they like you or not. So, let's pretend you said something funny about a television show that made everyone laugh. Within seconds, the person right next to you said the EXACT same thing so everyone

laughed again. But wait, the person next to him said the EXACT same thing you said and everyone laughed again. Finally, the girl next to him said almost the EXACT same thing that was already said three times and everyone laughed like they never heard you the very first time. I bet you would've stopped laughing a long time ago.

Well, teachers feel the same way. Sometimes they ask questions and students' answers sound like broken records (aka scratched albums or CDs — see Google again if you don't get it). **Your teachers are expecting you to show your brilliance instead**

of repeating what the text or another person has already said.

Good ideas are always welcome when they're original and unique. When a challenge or question seems impossible, that's the best time to come up with a bright idea. I had a student whose computer crashed before a due date. She typed her entire essay on her cell phone and went to a 24-hour office center to print. She met the deadline. This student refused to accept a bad solution. Her enterprising approach to overcoming challenges in high school prepared her to earn two degrees from a prestigious university and her dream job making $62 per hour.

But wait, there's more. I had another student who missed a few classes and an important lesson on the day before his 200-point project was due. Instead of begging for an extension, he contacted several peers to confirm the topic. He also explored Google to teach himself about the topic. This rockstar turned in an outstanding project on time. Now, he's a video game designer and traveling around the world.

I had yet another student who was too sick to come to school, but she had homework due that day. Instead of turning it in late, she surprised me by downloading an app onto her cell phone. This app allowed her to scan her handwritten 10+ pages (front and back), email the attachment, and share the pages

Middle School to the Max!

via Google Docs. She did all of this *before* school started to make sure that she beat the deadline from home.

Fast forward a few years, this same creative student graduated from high school with a 3.8 GPA and many awards. She also graduated from Penn State University and is wrapping up medical school to become a doctor. Her dreams since middle school are coming true. She's always been all action instead of all talk. This rockstar is going to earn six figures at a young age.

My last student story is one of my favorite stories of all time. My substitute teacher never showed up to my class. The kids didn't have an adult in the room. Instead of taking advantage of the situation, engaging in horseplay, being disruptive, catching up on sleep, or wasting a day, they came up with an impressive solution. The entire ninth grade class nominated three students to create six journal prompts (6+ paragraphs). These fourteen-year-olds in Cleveland, Ohio wrote more than 48 sentences in 45 minutes, stapled all of their work together, and delivered their paragraphs to the librarian.

Most of these former students graduated from high school and college with great grades. Others are high-ranking soldiers with multiple awards in the military or have very successful businesses. Now, they are making great money and traveling to gorgeous cities and countries like Egypt, Brazil, China, Mexico, Paris, Rome, Bora Bora, South Africa, Dubai, London, Japan, Spain, Thailand, Honduras, Morocco, Cuba, New Zealand, and Mozambique.

Of course, I love it when my students say or write powerfully original ideas. However, it's when my babies (students) come up with great ideas during a crisis that I want to hug them. *Thinking "outside the box" is thinking that's innovative, resourceful, or pure genius.* It's thinking that makes people see you as being pretty cool or the exception and not the norm. The only thing that can stop your brain from coming up with clever ideas is you. The brain loves chances to be innovative — the more the better.

Middle School to the Max!

Reflecting on Your High School Readiness

1) What are some synonyms for **creative**? Describe an incident when you should have been creative in how you responded to a difficult situation.

_____
_____
_____
_____

2) What do you need to do to be more **creative** (you know yourself best, so dig deep and keep it real with yourself)?

_____
_____
_____
_____

3) What was your *aha* moment while reading about this topic?

_____
_____
_____
_____

Bridget K. Lambright

High School Readiness Task

At the end of every topic, this section is for you to write down 3-5 important ideas that your future high school self will need your middle school self to remember.

Middle School to the Max!

Be a Problem – Solver

As you grow older, life will throw more and more situations your way that feel like impossible puzzles. If you haven't experienced this yet, just keep getting older. Eventually, you'll see what I mean. When you were younger, adults took care of everything for you. They made sure your life was easy and stress-free. They handled all of your challenges so you didn't have to worry about anything. **Life is starting to get complicated because the older you get, the more you're on your own.** Don't freak out, it's as natural as rain. For now, you just need to get good grades, pick good friends, be happy, respect your parents, and stay out of trouble.

As more responsibilities and choices are added to your life, the pressure may feel overwhelming.

I've taught hundreds of kids who just gave up or failed because they couldn't figure out where to put some of the perplexing pieces in their life's puzzle. **The EXACT moment a student gives up or**

gives in to making bad choices, he/she becomes a problem-maker.

Most kids don't realize it until they get caught or confronted, but just like a silent fart, the "funk" is in the air every time. Whether it's getting into a fight, arguing with an adult, defying rules, and skipping an assignment, a class, or school. Students who quit trying to do what's right are only making more problems for themselves. Some kids probably feel as though they should be able to do whatever they want, but they're rarely prepared for the harsh consequences.

Check this out, I've seen students get suspended, laugh about getting suspended, but still show up later at a school dance or game on the exact same day.  Please *make it make sense*! This also goes for banned students who skip too many classes all year. They still show up for their graduation. This is wild! It's all fun games for them until the adults have these suspended or banned students forcibly removed from the events...for trespassing. When it matters most, administrators don't usually let middle school students keep getting their way. In the end, these students always go from laughing about their situation to being super MAD. And that, my friend, is problem-maker energy!

I've been on planet Earth for over fifty years. I've met hundreds of kids and teenagers just like you. They've taught me some valuable life lessons. According to them, there isn't a problem you'll face in elementary, middle, or high school that you cannot figure out or get help with solving.

Nope, an UNsolvable problem does NOT exist at your age. No internet? Sick mama? No help at home? Getting bullied? No supplies? Homeless? Don't understand a topic? Feeling unloved? Falling behind? Stinky armpits? It doesn't matter. Don't play yourself. Please don't let a malfunction stop you from functioning. You have *all* the best answers in you or near you. Fyi, you know it's the best answer because it solves your problem instead of creating more problems for you or the people who love you. I know this is very harsh, but *life doesn't care* about your problems or preferences.

Deadlines will pass and new challenges will keep coming whether you keep up or not. So, stop waiting. Use your brain. Please get H-E-L-P before deadlines and due dates. Asking for help has *never* been a sign of weakness. Brave people ask for help all the time. They refuse to allow their fears to control their lives. Fear can be a dream destroyer. **Trust and believe,**

Bridget K. Lambright

good things don't always come to those who wait.

> Middle School to the Max!

Reflecting on Your High School Readiness:

1) What are the benefits of being a **problem solver** instead of a problem maker (don't just repeat the text)?

_____
_____
_____
_____

2) What do you need to do to be a better **problem solver** (you know yourself best, so dig deep and keep it real with yourself)?

_____
_____
_____
_____

3) What was your *aha* moment while reading about this topic?

_____
_____
_____
_____

Bridget K. Lambright

High School Readiness Task

At the end of every topic, this section is for you to write down 3-5 important ideas that your future high school self will need your middle school self to remember.

_____
_____
_____
_____
_____
_____
_____
_____
_____
_____

> Middle School to the Max!

Be a Visionary

Don't let anyone fool you. Real success doesn't come easy. That customary recognition where everyone gets a Participant's Award comes and goes. Getting away with cheating or lying comes and goes. But real success, where you are required to make sacrifices and give your best effort lasts a lifetime. If you already know that you're going to be a *doctor, lawyer, soldier, scientist, or entrepreneur, then you should see yourself in that medical coat, expensive suit, uniform, lab coat, or professional outfit* RIGHT NOW.

You don't have to wait to get older to imagine how you'll dress, what you'll drive, where you'll live, and who you'll marry. After you graduate from college, military training, or whatever else that's required, life is about **living** your dreams. A happy life is about controlling your own future. The more you have, the freer you are to live, eat, travel, and shop wherever you want. That might seem far away, but right now is the best time to be preparing for some of the best days of your life. **Every** time you look in a mirror, you need to see the success that you want to become in the future. Next, *walk, talk, think, and act like* the success you see every day in the mirror. Of course, I want you to fix your hair and get that food speck out of your teeth. Just don't forget to envision where you're headed.

Once you're on the right track, you need to stay put. If you earned awards in elementary school, keep earning them in middle school. Academic and Attendance awards still matter in high school. The more awards you earn in high school, there will be more opportunities set aside just for you. Jobs and colleges give awards to their hardest workers too. This recognition usually comes with money and/or free fancy trips to tropical places. Picture an audience clapping and cheering for you even when you're an adult.

Simply put, are you keeping your eye on the future prizes that Life has in store for you? If not, you could be jeopardizing the good that awaits you. We've all heard of Cancel Culture. Fortunately or unfortunately, it's a very real thing. I call it BYB (Burning Your Bag). Athletes are losing teams, fans, and endorsements — losing money. Students are losing out on college acceptances and scholarships — losing money.

Employees are losing their jobs — losing money. Even business owners are losing customers — losing money. One wrong move in middle or high school and your past could come back to block you from making really good money.

You don't want to do or say something inappropriate as a kid that a person could use against you when you're an adult (school records and online posts/pictures are permanent).

Recording and posting fights can be illegal. Sending pictures without wearing clothes is illegal. Bullying, threatening, or harassing someone on social media is illegal. Being in an unauthorized area is illegal. Destruction of property is illegal. Assaulting anyone is illegal. Some of those bad choices could get  parents or guardians sued and bank accounts snatched. I've met middle and high school students who thought that they were just being silly. They were wrong. There isn't a prank funny enough to go from trying to be a comedian to having to face the punishment. Missing out on a future dream opportunity or person hurts.

When adults go on trips, they typically use a GPS to plan their route and avoid getting lost. In the same way, picturing a happy future is like creating a mental GPS for your life. By envisioning where you want to go and what you want to achieve, you can create a roadmap for yourself that will guide you along the way. Plus, prevent you from losing your way in the present. **I have lots of old students who had big dreams, but they failed to create and execute the plan.** By doing things like failing classes, getting suspended, and/or even arrested, they messed up their futures before they even graduated from high school.

Sadly, I meet lots of kids who are all talk, but no action. They get blinded by their present instead of focusing on their future. However, I also have older students who are living the EXACT lives they envisioned or better lives than they could've ever imagined when they were your age. A few are even living a whole new world like Aladdin in the Disney movie. They avoided people, places, and situations that could mess up their vision.

Most of the choices you make right now will determine the trajectory of your *entire* future. This is like when a shooting star is headed in one direction but crashes into another star. Now the star's entire direction has been changed FOREVER. **One thing is certain: the shooting stars who make it to "infinity and beyond" are the stars who keep heading in the right direction.** So, please get in front of a mirror for a daily pep talk. Let yourself know that you believe in yourself. Look in your reflection's eyes, point your finger at your reflection's chest, and tell yourself, "If you can dream it, you can do it!"

Bridget K. Lambright

Reflecting on Your High School Readiness

1) What are some characteristics of *visionary* students?

_____
_____
_____
_____

2) Which of those characteristics do you need to work on (you know yourself best, so dig deep and keep it real with yourself)?

_____
_____
_____
_____

3) What was your *aha* moment while reading about this topic?

_____
_____
_____
_____

Middle School to the Max!

High School Readiness Task

At the end of every topic, this section is for you to write down 3-5 important ideas that your future high school self will need your middle school self to remember.

_____
_____
_____
_____
_____
_____
_____
_____
_____
_____

Bridget K. Lambright

Be Prepared

I bet that you're looking forward to going to your high school prom. Prom is a very important tradition just before graduation. The dress or tux, makeover with hairstyle or "fresh" cut, and limo or "raw" car usually cost hundreds to thousands of dollars. Some high schoolers start planning for prom in the ninth grade. It's weird how there are lots of seniors who are more excited about going to prom than graduating from high  school. Whew, I could say something about this, but I won't.

Prom and all its costly, time-consuming rituals are awesome, but they also prove a *very* important point. Every single one of you knows how to be impressive. Every single one of you knows how to plan and prepare for vital events. Every single one of you knows how to have high expectations. It also proves that your parents/guardians are willing to spend hundreds to thousands on things that are important to you. So what if prom isn't your *thing*? Maybe you play a sport or instrument. Maybe you have a gaming system or hobby. Perhaps it's all about your hair, clothes, and shoes. My point is that when it matters to you, the sky's the limit. Making sure that you get *exactly* what you want is all that matters.

These same planning skills that keep you happy in your personal life are critical to your academic life. Most of the *things* that are important to you today will not matter at all years from now. Even prom will be an old memory a few years after you graduate from high school. **But your grades are as immortal as the Greek gods.** I have students in their forties who still request their high school transcripts, recommendation letters, and help with getting better paying jobs. Teachers suddenly have amazing memories. They never forget which students came on time, prepared, and ready to learn versus those forgetful, tardy students who borrowed items or needed to go to their lockers and other classes to get items. **No one thinks you're ready to learn when you don't even bother to bring the right supplies.**

Bridget K. Lambright

Some high school teachers will require your family to buy supplies. It makes you look careless or defiant when you don't give yourself enough time to purchase the correct items. I guarantee that you'd be very upset and disappointed if your prom date showed up in the wrong outfit or color. Better yet, you might be one of those kids who'd be very unhappy if you gave your parents/guardians your birthday present list (gift list if you don't celebrate special days) and they replaced your requests with *their* choices instead of *your* choices.

In all seriousness, when it comes to some schools, your parents/guardians are responsible for buying and you're responsible for bringing the right supplies. In college, professors expect their students to bring the right supplies starting on *Day 1*. No one is sharing their supplies in college. Civilian occupations or the Army, Navy, Air Force, Marines, and Coast Guard don't want to hear excuses for being unprepared.

Just bringing whatever you feel like bringing to class makes as much sense as your stylist or barber cutting your hair with preschool scissors. If your family cannot afford the items, your teacher can plan **before** the deadline. It's your job to bring *all* of your supplies to class every day, no matter what.

Prom is cool, but colleges don't care about how you look or what you drive to prom. **They do care**

> Middle School to the Max!

about what your teachers have to say about you on your immortal report card. Employers do care about what your teachers have to say about you on your **References checklist.** Before colleges accept you or employers hire you, they want to find out from your teachers about your ability to come prepared for whatever they have planned.

Bridget K. Lambright

Reflecting on Your High School Readiness

1) What does being **prepared** have to do with proving your readiness to learn (don't just repeat the text)?

_____
_____
_____
_____

2) What do you need to do to be **prepared** EVERY single day (you know yourself best, so dig deep and keep it real with yourself)?

_____
_____
_____
_____
_____

3) What was your *aha* moment while reading about this topic?

_____
_____
_____
_____

Middle School to the Max!

High School Readiness Task

At the end of every topic, this section is for you to write down 3-5 important ideas that your future high school self will need your middle school self to remember.

_____
_____
_____
_____
_____
_____
_____
_____
_____

Bridget K. Lambright

Be Impressive

Have you ever considered what your expectations are when you get a haircut, eat at a restaurant, or shop at a store? Chances are, you expect your barber  or stylist to provide you with their best work, your waitress to get your order right, and your cashier to give you great customer service. And why shouldn't you have high expectations? After all, if you don't expect the best, you'll likely receive mediocre or even subpar service (treatment).

Unfortunately, not everyone delivers on these expectations. Some stylists make you wait for hours beyond your scheduled appointment time — as if your time isn't valuable. Some waiters and waitresses don't wash their hands after using the bathroom. Lots of cashiers will just throw your items in a bag without thanking you for spending your money where they work. *America would be a HOT MESS if no one cared about being impressive* or *The Best*. Just like it's important for your hair stylist, barber, waitress, cashier, or anyone else who's providing a service to meet or exceed your expectations, it's just as critical for you to meet or exceed your teachers' expectations.

You can impress your teachers by:

1) Asking the right questions.

It's not enough to ask a bunch of questions. You need to ask the best questions that will help you do your best.

2) Starting assignments immediately.

Begin working on Day One, while the directions and relevant information are still fresh in your head.

3) Getting feedback along the way.

Have enough of your work done so that you can receive constructive comments from your teacher days before the deadline.

4) Having the assignment completely ready before the due date to submit work early.

You cannot turn in some last-minute sloppy work and expect your teacher to be impressed. If you're still working on a homework assignment the same day that it's due,

Bridget K. Lambright

you ARE committing an academic sin (even if you're just writing your name or needing to staple).

Middle school is where you **master the art** of meeting and exceeding your future high school teachers', college professors', and bosses' expectations. You never know who's watching you.

One day, I was visiting a school while these mean girls were teasing a crying girl during lunch. They were throwing food at her and calling her nasty names. Before I could intervene, a male student removed her from the nearby table, took her aside, talked to her until she stopped crying, and reported the bullies. His courageous actions were impressive. If you had to choose between hiring the unimpressive girls and the impressive boy for a job that pays $80 per hour (most jobs have an eight-hour day), which student is going to get your $640 per day?

When teachers don't demand your best, then they put you at risk of becoming a struggling high school student who constantly makes goofy mistakes, argues with teachers, terrorizes others, or disrupts learning. Thousands of high school teachers, professors, and employers have been frustrated with middle schools for the last few decades. But, wait a minute! I wrote this manual because I'm sick of professors and employers thinking that most teachers don't have high expectations.

Teachers work for one hundred million taxpayers. Taxpayers pay educators to prepare students (you) for the demands of the real world. True, you're already living in the real world. But, the world gets *very* real (gloves off) after high school.

FYI, teachers are taxpayers too. You're growing up in a demanding country where everyone who refuses to meet taxpayers' expectations ends up struggling on the bottom. Whereas, students who exceed expectations are given all the great opportunities. In case you haven't noticed, there are millions and millions of adults on the bottom rung of America's economic ladder. Most are stuck like Chuck. If you stay focused in elementary, middle, and high school, you increase your odds of getting picked for a job that pays very well with benefits. Most companies that pay really good money only recruit, hire, or promote the best of the best.

In colleges and universities, there are professors who will not touch wrinkled papers or will give you an

automatic zero on a 10-page paper because you make one silly mistake. And nope, they won't let you fix your careless mistake. Plus, you're mistaken if you believe that your mommy or daddy can force a professor to accept what teachers accept (to be nice). It's illegal for professors to even talk about your work with your parents because college students are adults.

Your teachers may accept some mistakes for now, but don't get too comfortable. To permit is to promote. Be grateful if you have a teacher, school, and school district that promotes excellence. It may be exhausting now, but the demands are getting you ready to excel in the workplace, the military, or college. Before long, being impressive will come naturally and the pressure won't feel so bad.

Students who refuse to practice being impressive are in for a rude awakening. They usually grow up into tired, bitter adults who work super hard on jobs they hate. Their payday doesn't matter because they never earn enough money to pay bills and enjoy life to the fullest. **Make no mistake, some of the highest-paying jobs are very demanding.**

School is where you give your teachers what they want in order to get what you need. Doors (opportunities) will open for you that you didn't even know about. People like to say that you can't miss what you never had. Yeah, good luck with that. Once you see someone else having an amazing experience, you can't unsee it. Most of us waste our precious minutes, hours, or days watching others. It's human nature to want what they have. However, our time should be spent building our own dream lives. When you make a habit of meeting and exceeding expectations, you'll never have to worry about struggling on the bottom or being just a spectator.

*Agreeable impression = smile, on time, neat appearance, confident handshake, polite demeanor, eye contact, etc.

Reflecting on Your High School Readiness

1) In what way does being *impressive* and excelling in school prepare you for adulthood?
___
___
___
___

2) What do you need to do to be *impressive* in your classes (you know yourself best, so dig deep and keep it real with yourself)?
___
___
___
___

3) What was your *aha* moment while reading about this topic?
___
___
___
___

Middle School to the Max!

High School Readiness Task

At the end of every topic, this section is for you to write down 3-5 important ideas that your future high school self will need your middle school self to remember.

_____
_____
_____
_____
_____
_____
_____
_____
_____
_____

Bridget K. Lambright

Be Prompt

Once upon a time, I worked for a principal who  was in charge of one of the highest-ranked schools in Ohio. His students had some of the best scores. There was even a waiting list for students who wanted to be accepted into this elite high school. Every applicant was rigorously tested and interviewed before being accepted. These kids were on a mission to become doctors or scientists.

Every teacher was personally responsible for their students' successes or failures. One day this principal held a training session for teachers. He stressed how his teachers were teaching the best kids, so he hired the best and expected our very best. He went on to say that one way to give our best was to start teaching as soon as the bell rang. At first, I thought this was a strange hill to plant his flag (non-negotiable opinion), but then he put some numbers up on the whiteboard.

Middle School to the Max!

Did you know that if a teacher waited just 1-2 minutes every day for students to unpack and greet their neighbors, they would be wasting 195-390 minutes per school year? That's equivalent to 3 to more than 6 hours of lost teaching time and taxpayer money down the drain.

Imagine if you were my boss and paid me $50 per hour, but I made you wait a couple of minutes every single day before I started working. That would be like I'm stealing $150 to $300 a year from your pocket. And if that wasn't bad enough, what if I also took bathroom breaks whenever I felt like it instead of waiting for my designated break time? Let's see…it takes about five minutes to use the potty (assuming you want me to wash my hands).

I'll probably go at a time when you really need me to be working…at least two times a week. So, that's 10 minutes per week out of 39 weeks a year, which equals 390 WASTED minutes for the year. **So, that's more than 6 hours to use the bathroom when it's not my break.** Again, you pay me $50 an hour.

So, now I'm also stealing more than $300 a year to go to the bathroom when I should be working for you. Now, combine the $150-$300 that I'd steal by making you wait at the beginning of class with the more than $300 that I'd steal by going to the bathroom whenever I felt the urge. Whew! I'm *hitting*

Bridget K. Lambright

your pockets for $450 to $600 per year. I've been teaching for 27 years so I've stolen $16,200. Now, multiply that madness by five because other employees are going to copy me after they see that you let me get away with stealing your time and money. I'm not even going to include the time and money being stolen whenever I stop teaching before the bell rings.

For my own sake, I hope that you'd fire me. Just give the job to someone who is ready to give you his/her best as soon as the clock starts. An impressive employee would train his/her bladder to wait until a break. If you wouldn't want an employee who steals  money from you, then don't be a student who steals time from the class (and money from taxpayers). It costs over $15,000 a year to educate you. Hello-o-o! School isn't free! Someone has to pay for the books, computers, copiers, paper, buildings, software, utilities, desks, faculty, staff, etc. Your parents pay a very small portion of what goes towards your public or charter school education. The majority of your "free" education from kindergarten thru 12th grade is paid for by millions of complete strangers (taxpayers).

In other words, y-o-u cost taxpayers and businesses almost $200,000 on your way to an education. That's why every moment in a classroom is as precious as gold. Every minute costs someone something. Now you see why taxpayers have a right to get mad when more students aren't graduating from high school. They want a return on their investment after paying for your education.

You'd be mad too if you worked hard and were forced to pay for a really expensive device, but the box was empty when you opened it. Plus, you couldn't get your money back! Plus, plus, you have to pay for the same empty box every April (tax month) until you die! Millions of taxpayers don't even have kids, but they still must pay for your education.

Wow, still don't think that a student should have to *hold it*? Then look at it this way: students are not invisible. Every person is a *huge* distraction whenever he/she enters or leaves a classroom. The teacher must stop just to hear a request, process a response, give permission, write a hall pass, and stop to repeat details when someone returns. Plus, once one person goes, then it becomes a Potty Party. **Going to the bathroom is what I call a P.P. or Personal Problem.** Class time is not the time to deal with personal problems. When you make your personal problem a class problem, you end up wasting precious time that you and your classmates can **never** get back. Every minute counts when it comes to learning and acquiring knowledge. Once you miss out on something in middle or high school, you can never go back to get it. **What's done cannot be undone.**

My best students over the years arrived early to get a front-row seat, unpacked early, quickly set up their supplies, were ready to work as soon as the bell rang, and rarely asked to go to the bathroom. They never had problems with missed directions because they never left the room. The last *thing* on their minds was talking to their friends or moving slowly before the bell. They trained their bladders to go before class or held the urge to go to the bathroom until after class. These same students also graduated from high school and college with honors and awards. They always impressed their professors with their self-control and focus.

You want to get on your teacher's, professor's, or boss' bad side? Walk in and out while he/she is talking. Hopefully, you won't get locked out. Better yet, ask him/her to slow down, wait on you, and repeat what you missed. Just don't be surprised if your professor ignores you when you raise your hand. Professors and employers DON'T play. They don't have to cater to your every need. When they ask a

> Middle School to the Max!

student/employee to leave or send for security to have someone removed, this usually means that the student/employee can *never* return to the room (no refunds or wages).

I keep trying to tell you that colleges and companies don't play by the same rules as your elementary, middle, or high school. I know I sound like a broken record. There's a reason why high school graduates drop out of college, workers get fired from good jobs, or soldiers get dishonorably discharged. **Sometimes you must put bad habits aside when they make you look like you're ready for daycare instead of high school.**

Bridget K. Lambright

Reflecting on Your High School Readiness

1) If you were paid lots of cash to **arrive early**, get set-up quickly, avoid absences, remain in class, etc., how would you use or treat your time in class (don't just repeat the text)?

_____
_____
_____
_____

2) What do you need to do to be *early*, ready, and in class the entire time (you know yourself best, so dig deep and keep it real with yourself)?

_____
_____
_____
_____

3) What was your *aha* moment while reading about this topic?

_____
_____
_____
_____

Middle School to the Max!

High School Readiness Task

At the end of every topic, this section is for you to write down 3-5 important ideas that your future high school self will need your middle school self to remember.

_____
_____
_____
_____
_____
_____
_____
_____
_____
_____

Bridget K. Lambright

Be an Active Listener

For over twenty-five years, I've been preparing students for their college graduations and future careers. As a teacher, it's important to me that my students are fully aware of the demands and challenges they will face. If a student drops out of college or gets fired from a job, he/she can never say that I didn't warn him/her.

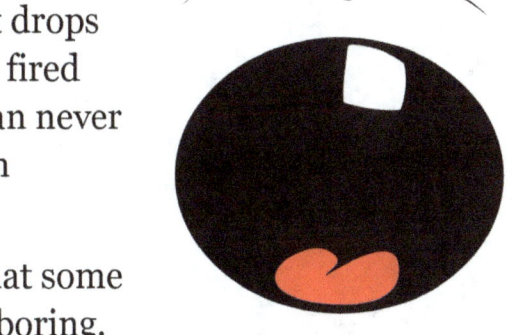

You may think that some of your teachers are boring. Trust me, they're nothing compared to some professors and bosses. These individuals can talk for hours on end and some voices can sound like nothing more than "blah, blah, blah, blah." **If you're not careful, you'll wake up in a puddle of warm drool.** A few instructors may be interesting, but listening to most college lectures and work meetings are as boring as watching worms crawl on pavement. When your teacher's lesson is boring, you'll need to turn on your laser-sharp focusing skills. Have you ever thought about how paying attention to adults must be very important since we have two eyes and two ears? Notice how you only have one mouth?

When a teacher is boring, it can be tempting to tune out or fall asleep. Snoozing is the easy choice. But doing so can easily result in falling behind or even failing. Choosing easy is rarely a good idea.

As someone who visits schools frequently, I've seen my fair share of sleeping students. Their snoring is always amusing. Watching them fall further behind is always tragic.

Many students have told me that they only stay awake during games like Kahoot or Blooket. While I understand the desire to be entertained, it's not realistic to expect every class to be fun and games. When teachers focus solely on entertainment, it can set students up for failure. They are being trained to believe that learning is always supposed to be fun. Their brains will refuse to engage in any subject that isn't entertaining.

It's important to remember that not all learning can be entertaining, but it's necessary for growth and development. While teachers may try to make lessons interesting and engaging, it's not feasible to expect that every minute of the day will be entertaining. High school is not an amusement park. Not every course or teacher will be enjoyable.

Sometimes a subject is serious or too hard to grasp for fun and games. My dad used to say that he didn't send me to school to make friends or have fun. He sent me to school to get my education and do something with my life. Thanks Daddy, because so far, so good. I never expected my teachers to entertain me. I wasn't surprised when my professors didn't. You need to learn how to entertain yourself. Keep count of how many times your teacher says certain vocabulary words or key terms. If there aren't any pictures to help you, make your own graphic organizers while listening. **It also helps to sit straight up in your seat with your feet firmly planted on the ground while constantly taking notes.**

When you start to feel sleepy, underline important notes. Draw a picture that represents the notes. My daughter has struggled with having ADHD for her entire life. She's grown and still has to work really hard to pay attention. Please search Google or ask for help with paying attention. Don't get me wrong, your teachers should try to be entertaining or interesting most days of the week. Smiling and learning go together like peanut butter and jelly. You're still young with only a few years left to be a kid. However, the responsibility for learning as much as humanly possible is on you.

Hopefully, the day will come when you'll be in (boring) meetings while you're making lots of money at your dream job. That's why *now* is the time to learn how to stay focused. Whatever  you need to do, please make sure to perfect the skill of maintaining eye contact with the speaker while looking interested and engaged. This posture communicates that you're positive, serious, and committed to achieving your goals such as earning an A.

Bridget K. Lambright

Reflecting on Your High School Readiness

1) What do most students do when they get sleepy in your classes (don't just repeat the text)?

_____
_____
_____
_____

2) What do you need to do to **actively listen** even though you're bored (you know yourself best, so dig deep and keep it real with yourself)?

_____
_____
_____
_____

3) What was your *aha* moment while reading about this topic?

_____
_____
_____
_____

Middle School to the Max!

High School Readiness Task

At the end of every topic, this section is for you to write down 3-5 important ideas that your future high school self will need your middle school self to remember.

_____
_____
_____
_____
_____
_____
_____
_____
_____
_____

Bridget K. Lambright

Be a Writer

Bad writing is like bad breath. One hurts the eyes and the other hurts the nose. When you write, your goal should be to impress and not just get it done. **Your writing represents who you are and all that you stand for.** Careless writing makes you look careless. Awesome writing makes you look awesome. How do you want your teachers to see you? Teachers know in the first sentence if your work will be "fire" or lame. He/She is either going to read your work because he/she wants to or is being forced. As the writer, you should know what tone, style, and words to use so that your writing is "lit" (very good).

Thousands of middle school students go to high schools with poor writing skills. Their high schools send them to college or work with these same weak skills. Did you know that colleges had to create remedial classes because too many freshmen have poor reading and writing skills? These classes are only for students who didn't learn what they should have learned in middle and high school. Sometimes in elementary, middle, and high school, administrators or teachers try to sugarcoat (say things nicely) data. They don't want kids and parents to feel bad/mad when hearing the truth. Here's a *harsh* truth, the dropout rate is higher for students who get frustrated with being behind. **When you get what you need from middle school, then you won't need remedial assignments in high school or as an adult.**

It's sad, because on the flipside, really good young writers can be placed into a high school's Honors English, CCP, or Advanced Placement classes. In college, really good writers can be exempt from Freshman English classes. I've even had professors hire some of my past students to grade papers for them. I want that success story to be *you*.

In college, remedial classes aren't free and don't count toward graduation. **Some colleges won't let you use your financial aid to pay for remedial classes because you should've used your precious time in middle and high school.** So how do you avoid writing below your grade level, needing remedial lessons, being placed in a remedial class in college, or making your boss laugh at you?

Bridget K. Lambright

Pay attention to any educator who gives you feedback regarding your writing skills. It takes concern and lots of time to give each student constructive comments.

Please don't be a student who ignores the feedback. There's nothing wrong with getting frustrated. There's nothing right with giving up. If you don't make the suggested changes, your teacher may think that you don't care. Some teachers only care as much as their students care. If you do make improvements, then he/she will keep helping you get better. You'll need to follow directions, study the rubric, ask for graded examples, get help, turn in every assignment, and embrace the teacher's feedback to get better every day.

Reading lots of books about topics you're interested in is important too. Readers read writing and writers write reading. Most good writers become good because they're readers too. When your teacher is reading your work, he/she is being a reader. It's his/her job to give you praise and/or pointers. Your teacher isn't telling you to fix your work because he/she doesn't like you. As a matter of fact, *any teacher who lets you misspell words, use incorrect punctuation, accepts copied or AI generated content (plagiarism), ignores run-ons or fragments, and doesn't require original, well-developed paragraphs* **truly doesn't care about your future** *(far worse than not liking you)*.

Middle School to the Max!

Here are my <u>Rockstar Writing Rules</u> that have helped my students rise above their peers in high school and college:

- **Never** write the same way that you speak or text.
- Stop using terms such as "thing", "something", "nothing", "everything", "anything", and "stuff" when you write for school, because it's overused, weak, boring, vague, and potentially confusing.
- Have a professional instead of a "my buddy" mindset while writing in school. Use third-person pronouns (he, she, they, them). Avoid first- or second-person pronouns.
- Try not to start your sentences with "or", "to", "and", "because", "with", "that", "but", "then", "without", "what", "where", "why",

"how", "did", "who", "being", "not", "by", etc. Think about what you're trying to say and flip the words around. Writing is playing chess with words. The goal is to express your idea in the best way possible.

- **After middle school, stop repeating the prompt in your opening or closing because it's annoying and repetitive.** Repeating the prompt was a crutch to get you started, but using crutches forever is not healthy.
- Make sure that you start every paragraph with a main point and "break" that point down (analysis).
- Keep your definitions to yourself because it's insulting to define words for educated readers.
- Learn writing rules, memorize sentence patterns (8), use a variety of sentence patterns, and thoroughly develop every idea.
- Make sure that you know the basic MLA and APA rules instead of depending on online

tools or software programs to cite sources for you (back to Google again). If you use a program to input bibliographic information without knowing the basic rules, you're guaranteed to make careless mistakes that'll damage your essay's credibility. **No one wants to read a poorly formatted paper.** It's like having someone who never brushes his/her teeth blow his/her funky breath into your nose. Ignorance is never a good excuse when it comes to your work and grade. Remember, you can't blame a citation program for your failure to follow the rules. Just like I can't blame my car's cruise control for going 70 mph in a 55 mph zone.

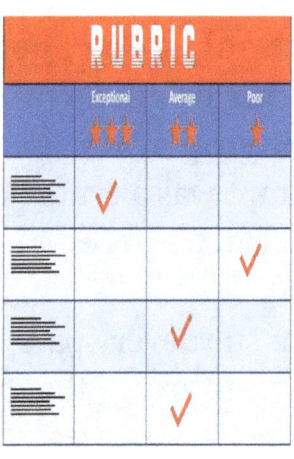

- Your essays must give credit to sources that help you (a little or a lot) when you write.
- Make sure that you address the prompt instead of writing off-topic or arguing both sides. Pick one position to defend or prove.

Bridget K. Lambright

- **You should not be writing the same way in middle school as you wrote in elementary school. The same rule applies when you get to high school. The same rule applies when you go to college, work, or the military.** Your sentences and paragraphs should be much longer. The vocabulary you use should make you sound more mature and knowledgeable with each passing grade level.
- Make sure you only use punctuation when you're positive about the rule.
- Lastly, your analytical sentences should be impressive and not awkward or unbearable to read.

If you don't like to read or write, then you're not alone. I teach lots of students who just want to write three to five measly sentences. It's obvious that they just rushed to get it done. Ow, my eyes! My eyes! Only the best  writers can give an awesome explanation in four sentences. The rest of us must write like we're miners digging for diamonds. Every sentence is a layer that brings us closer to striking it rich. If you already have an "A" in your middle or high school English class, these tips are still for you too. When I was a high school English teacher, I met students who always earned great grades in middle school, but their writing still wasn't so good. They'd be so mad at me until they started to improve. Now, we laugh about their struggles. It's not just about the grades you received, but the skills you have!

I know this topic is too long, but let me tell you that being a good reader and writer is essential for life. Your future children will need a mommy or daddy who knows how to write a powerful, error-free complaint letter.

The pen is mightier than the sword (Edward Bulwer-Lytton in 1839). *Some people resort to cursing and fighting because they cannot write a compelling letter.* Teachers require students to write a lot because that's all you'll do in college and on some good-paying jobs. If you have your own business, you'll write letters to clients, banks, partners, and other businesses. Almost every college class requires essays. You'll have to write so much that your fingers will cramp and your brain will want to shut down.

But you cannot stop because your future depends on your writing skills, reading skills, and determination. Sometimes you'll have timed writing that requires more than ten paragraphs during a class. No, you won't get extra time. That's why now is the time to practice.

Reading and writing every summer will help you keep those skills or you'll lose them. Your parents may need to hire an ELA tutor because teachers can only do so much. Remember, if you master your skills right now, you won't need remedial lessons in high school or be placed in a college's remedial English course. You don't want your future

bosses or coworkers laughing at your emails and letters behind your back. When your teachers use a red pen or write suggestions, please fix every mistake. *They're trying to save your writing from being mediocre or worse.*

Rewrites are merciful gifts that some teachers and most professors do not have to give. Practice is the *only* strategy that makes perfect. Research states that it takes thousands of hours of deliberate practice to master a skill. The more that you practice writing, the less painful the process. Writing always has been and always will be an important way to communicate your intelligence and feelings.

> Middle School to the Max!

    I know that I'm biased because I've always adored Language Arts. However, it wasn't until my former students became the first person in their families to graduate from college with one or more Bachelor's and Master's degrees that I witnessed its power. Many other former students are running their own successful businesses too. Now, their kids are graduating from high school using the same tips that I taught their parents.

    Strong reading and writing skills can change your *entire* life. Even the world's richest celebrities, Rihanna, Michael Jordan, Oprah Winfrey, Jay-Z, Diddy, LeBron James, and Tyler Perry credited their teachers for their successes. Have you ever noticed how these *self-made* billionaires are now enjoying the goodies that can come from taking advantage of a "free" education? Some of my former students are working on their 100-page dissertations (essays) to earn a doctorate. How would your last name sound with Dr. in front of it? I want you to stand in a mirror and say it aloud a few times. Yeah, Dr. _____ has a nice ring to it. **If you're a good reader and writer, then you're unstoppable!**

Bridget K. Lambright

Reflecting on Your High School Readiness

1) What is your attitude about any **reading or writing** assignment?

_____
_____
_____
_____

2) What do you need to do to be a better **writer** and **reader** (you know yourself best, so dig deep and keep it real with yourself)?

_____
_____
_____
_____

3) What was your *aha* moment while reading about this topic?

_____
_____
_____
_____

Middle School to the Max!

High School Readiness Task

At the end of every topic, this section is for you to write down 3-5 important ideas that your future high school self will need your middle school self to remember.

_____
_____
_____
_____
_____
_____
_____
_____
_____

Bridget K. Lambright

Be Cooperative

Since I'm still visiting classrooms, I get to see and hear what kids are thinking, doing, and feeling. I've been listening to students for twenty-seven years. Actually, I've been listening to students for over forty years, if you include the time when I was a student. Yes, I was a kid just like you a long, long, long time ago. I sat at hard desks, carried heavy backpacks, ate nasty lunches, ran to classes, listened to boring teachers, complained about everybody, and did countless hours of homework. Most nights, I barely slept because I wanted really good grades. Schools haven't changed much. Now, I'm on the other side of the mountain. A mountain that you're just beginning to climb. I don't envy you.

One of the saddest facts about school is that there are some classrooms, hallways, and even entire schools that are filled with negative energy caused by negative kids. It's not something that anyone likes to talk about, but it's true. As an adult, I'm constantly shocked by the hundreds of students I encounter who use some truly naughty words and have some very inappropriate conversations. Sometimes the words and topics are so bad that I can't help but wonder how these kids kiss their parents. Their lips are pushing out such shockingly dirty statements.

Now, I don't know if I'm talking about you specifically. If I am, then I want you to know that you're not alone. It's going to be a rough ride. You can handle it. You just need to buckle up and prepare yourself for the journey ahead. When negative behaviors become too intense, they make teaching and learning a challenge. We all know that it only takes one disrespectful kid in a class to bring teaching to a complete stop. So, it makes sense that if there are lots of disrespectful, disruptive kids in a class together, learning could be replaced with chaos.

For whatever reason, there are kids who'll come to a place of learning (school) to be the main ones who stop learning from happening. **That's like you going to the bathroom and a student following you into the stall to be the main one who stops you from urinating.** Schools, like bathrooms, serve an important purpose. Anyone who gets in the way is DEAD WRONG. Environments must be kept conducive for learning or *it's a wrap*. On a side note, I really hope that you're one of the good ones. If you have to ask your teacher, then you're a problem.

Bridget K. Lambright

Uh-oh, I'm keeping it really real!

A few years back, I had the privilege of helping to launch a program that allowed high-achieving students to attend a university. They were still juniors in high school. It was an incredible opportunity for these college-ready kids. The results were astounding. Every single student in the program told us that they loved being on the college campus. Everyone they encountered was so nice and positive. It was a stark contrast to what they experienced in their high school. Profanity, gossiping, fights, thefts, arguing, threats, and disruptions were all too common.

In fact, these bright, young students described their high school as the antithesis of the heavenly college campus. It's hard to imagine how disheartening that must have been for them. This is a sad reality that too many high school students throughout America must endure. These sixteen-year-olds preferred being surrounded by adults  in a college setting just to avoid the hot-mess behaviors that ran rampant in their high school.

It's a shame that high schools can be such toxic environments for students who are eager to learn and grow. But it's inspiring to see how these college-ready kids were able to rise above it all. They thrived in an

atmosphere that encouraged positivity and growth. It just goes to show that when given the opportunity, young people are capable of achieving incredible things.

College isn't a perfect world. But during learning hours, almost every student behaves as if he/she is a scholar and destined for success. Students don't groom themselves during class, argue with others, or deliberately disrupt learning with loud talking in hallways and classrooms. They avoid these inappropriate behaviors. Doing otherwise would be downright *creepy*.

College students are usually an ambitious group. They arrive in their classes with their eyes fixed firmly on the prize: a quality education that will set them up for success. For these driven students, time is money. They're eager to dive headfirst into their studies.

Unfortunately, not every student shares this mindset. Disrespectful or disruptive behaviors can derail a class and rob dedicated students of the education they've paid for. It's no surprise that many students get angry when this happens. They're investing their time and money in their education. They expect to get their money's worth.

In fact, some colleges are so serious about maintaining a positive and respectful environment that they have strict codes of conduct in place. These schools are known for their rigorous academic programs. They also demand that their students behave in a manner that is in line with their high standards. It's very hard to get accepted into these elite institutions. However, students who are up to the challenge gain access to tremendous rewards. You need to know that college students go to campus every day focused on handling their business. *If you're one of the good kids in your classes, then I'm talking about you. You're not even in college yet, so keep up the good work.*

College isn't free. It's silly to waste the opportunity. Students in college want to be impressive. Their goal is to get picked for opportunities and recognized for their excellence.

Professors won't write recommendation letters for negative students whose behaviors block teaching and learning. Selective (careful) employers ignore college graduates who can't get outstanding recommendations from their professors. Commanders in the military won't tolerate insubordination too. Practically everyone in college is there for the right reasons. They want to earn great grades, graduate, and get an awesome job. These are the same reasons why elementary, middle, and high school students should behave like scholars. Time is still cash money. **Your school prepares you for college, work, and the military.**

The students that I mentioned earlier earned over $300,000 in college while they were still in high school. Since elementary school, these same students constantly behaved as though they were college-ready scholars. Before they graduated from college, they shared their pictures of being seated in the front row *before* the professor arrived. I felt like a proud mama! Now **100 percent of these scholars** are doing exactly what they said they always wanted to do when I first met them as fourteen year olds. They're college graduates and earning amazing money while traveling around the world. **Sadly, 70 percent of the disruptive, disrespectful kids** who were also in the program never made it to college or gainful employment. Most are already facing a hard, cruel world. They made some reckless choices at your age and continued on this path throughout high school. Remember what I said about habits?

High schools want good people around. Everyone learns better in positive environments. I've worked with some of the most intelligent students who didn't know how to disagree without losing their tempers.

Their eyes would start rolling, lips start smacking, and voices became too loud for the space. They would take class discussions personally. Some kids were so upset that they seemed ready to fight…over a topic. In

the adult world (not reality TV world), people look down on adults who start screaming and yelling during a discussion.

Aggressiveness makes people in any college, branch of the military, or at work want to **avoid** a "heated" person. If you want to be heard, allow your intelligence to speak louder than your voice. *Learning is hard enough without adding disrespectful or disruptive behaviors into the mix.* A compliant attitude will take you so much farther in life than an argumentative attitude. Your lips speak what's in your heart. If you have a positive heart, then you'll speak *goodness*. If you have a negative heart, then you'll speak *badness*. Right now, **your mouth** is either helping or hindering learning in every class. Right

> Middle School to the Max!

now, **your presence** is making your school the place to be or not to be.

Some EXCELLENT teachers have quit teaching or become weary and sick because of rude, defiant, and lazy kids. Teachers go to college to learn how to prepare you for high school, college, and a career. They would rather focus on teaching instead of policing. *Schools that have the best ratings, scores, reputations, and college acceptance rates are FILLED with kids who allow teachers to do their job without major interruptions.* Since every student shapes a school's reputation, you're more important than you realize.

Did you know that teachers are miserable when misbehaviors stop them from doing what they love? A friend told me about a talented teacher who quit teaching. He became a septic tank driver (hauls 5,000 gallons of tee-tee and turds from toilets every day) because his students were so disrespectful, rude, and lazy. I know the story is true. I've visited wild classes where I wouldn't have made it twenty minutes let alone twenty years.

Bridget K. Lambright

These students' antics were way more disgusting than hauling human urine and boo-boo for a living. They were hurting their futures, classroom community, school's reputation, and ability to positively contribute to America. I felt horrible for the scholars who came to class to learn. They were trapped! When I asked some disruptive students about their lack of self-control, they always blamed the teacher. *Um, the magic word in self-control is self.*

Luckily, the best teachers can just take their talents elsewhere, like when a really good player leaves a struggling team. But we all know what happens to teams when all the BEST players **shut down or leave.** It's usually the die-hard fans and city who suffer the most. Deservedly, life ALWAYS gives negative kids a big *payback* as adults that's NEVER pretty (low wages, back-breaking jobs, rude bosses, warrants, troublesome offspring, inconsistent employment, violent environments, disloyalty, no transportation, financial dependency, disrespectful customers, heartbreaking relationships, revoked licenses, and whatever else they earned).

Karma has a cousin named Destiny. When these two have had enough, it's crazy to watch these cousins reciprocate past misdeeds. They always find a way to render justice. You may not believe in Karma, but Karma believes in you. How do I know how Karma works?! Well, I have more than 700 former students in their 20s, 30s, and 40s as Facebook friends/acquaintances. I could have hundreds more FB friends, but some ex-students were just too defiant as kids. I reject their requests.

My point is that I'm using their 700 lives to warn you about what's ahead in your future. Your behavior and attitude will determine your future too. Right now, they're living through one or more of the bad situations I just mentioned. On the flipside, the former students who made their schools a better place with their positive presence aren't getting clobbered by Karma. Their lives are so beautifully blessed that I wish we were neighbors. Content people make the world a happier place. Go back and take a look at the *MAXimize Your Future Salary* chart (see page 61).

It's not rocket science. Your attitude, vibe, and mentality will make or break you. They'll have a greater impact on your future than your intelligence. **If you don't know that you *will* always reap as an adult what you sowed as a kid, then you better ask somebody.** Every single day, I get to see former students whining about their misery or celebrating their happiness. Keep in mind that you're an adult much longer than you're a kid. *Your bitter or sweet payback will last for more than* **SIXTY YEARS**. That's a very, very long time to suffer or celebrate.

In just a few years, your high school teachers will write recommendation letters just like professors in college. If you're already a high school-ready student, then you can ask **any** teacher to write a recommendation letter or submit your name for an opportunity because you have a good reputation.

Middle School to the Max!

When there are special programs for a limited number of middle school students, the sponsors and organizers *only* want the names of impressive scholars.

Hopefully, they'd want you. When you're in high school, you'll need recommendation letters for job, internship, volunteer, or scholarship opportunities too. **If you can't ask your core teachers to write letters for you, you need to change your attitude immediately.** Students with great letters have better choices. Students with weak letters must hope that there are extra spots left over for them.

I've had insubordinate students who needed letters to stay out of jail. Are you vouching for someone who's nasty and disrespectful towards you?

That's why you want to embrace good behaviors, so they become good habits. It's logical to help polite people. Kids who believe it's completely normal to refuse to sit down and be quiet, argue with teachers, lie about teachers, make teachers and students cry, be destructive, steal others' items, get in fights, or worse are **wrong on so many different levels!**

Every country on earth finds these kids repugnant (yuckier than a big, slimy green-yellow booger stuck to a light switch). Our society cannot wait to press the *Reject* button on young adults who can't get it together through middle school and high school. Several states are building billion-dollar prisons to prepare for all those insubordinate kids who aren't on track to graduate from high school (see Google). Since numbers don't lie, states must prepare for the next flood of statistics!

Right about now, there are probably some students who are thinking that I'm not telling the truth. Here's my reply to them. I don't have any reason to be a fibber. Think about it. I'm just an old lady who has seen *a lot* of heartbroken adults in avoidable situations. Disorderly kids grow up to become trouble and danger magnets. Some of you know I'm right. Honestly, I have a desperate reason to tell you the awful truth. I'm afraid *for* you.

Fear is a powerful motivator. Now, would probably be a good time to share Fact #5 about high school dropouts. **Their life expectancy is six to nine years *less* than high school and college graduates.*** Juvenile detention centers and cemeteries are full of bright, stubborn kids. So, when kids curse out teachers and think they've won, I'm sad for them. They don't understand. The teacher is the real MVP for keeping calm. He/She has already graduated from college with skills, achieved a good job with benefits, and will receive sympathy from fellow teachers. Most importantly, every disrespected teacher is predicted to *outlive* disrespectful dropouts.

Please...please...please use your time in middle school and high school to get really good at being respectful and professional.

I highly suggest sitting down with your teachers to discuss where you stand based upon my high school readiness survey. Now is the time to make sure that you're headed in the right direction. It's never good to assume. **You're. Never. Too. Old. To. Change.** It's very important to be impressive in all the areas that I discuss in this manual. **High schools, colleges, and businesses will believe your teachers before they believe you.**

*https://www.richmondfed.org/publications/research/econ_focus/2014/q3/feature1

Bridget K. Lambright

Reflecting on Your High School Readiness

1) Describe your heart (attitude) when it comes to school and learning.

_____
_____
_____
_____

2) What do you need to do to have a better attitude and be a positive force in your school (you know yourself best, so dig deep and keep it real with yourself)?

_____
_____
_____
_____

3) What was your *aha* moment while reading about this topic?

_____
_____
_____
_____

Middle School to the Max!

High School Readiness Task

At the end of every topic, this section is for you to write down 3-5 important ideas that your future high school self will need your middle school self to remember.

_____
_____
_____
_____
_____
_____
_____
_____
_____

Bridget K. Lambright

Be Engaged

If you still don't know why you need to turn off *and* stow your electronic devices after all these tips that I've been sharing, then I've failed you. **You can't focus 100 percent on getting ready for high school when you're distracted.** Research has proven that music, videos, games, and people can interrupt your brain. Some kids get so pumped that they interrupt teaching and learning. They are either loudly rapping in the halls or cursing and fighting because of a social media post. Schools have rules about electronic devices to eliminate unnecessary distractions.

Remember, time is money. You can't come back to learn what you've missed. Adults usually have to pay to learn what you're learning right now…for "free". Millions cannot afford to pay the fees or don't have reliable transportation and free time because of their low wage job. Rules can be very annoying. However, they exist to help or protect you.

Middle School to the Max!

There would be dangerous chaos in our society without rules.

How would you feel if everyone was living his/her best life on a cell phone or enjoying movies/games at your loved one's funeral? Maybe you're so laid back that cell phones wouldn't bother you at your family's funeral. Maybe you'd be bothered if your doctor was busy texting and posting while you're having a bad asthma attack. A surgeon was recently disciplined for riding his hoverboard and taking selfies with an unconscious patient during her surgery. **The reality is that cellphone use in some settings is disrespectful, dangerous, or unprofessional.**

It's important to be honest with yourself. You would want everyone's undivided attention when you have an important activity or need. One of the most crucial activities in life is *learning*. That's why it's essential to give your teachers and classmates your undivided attention during class. When you're distracted, you miss out on the opportunity to learn how to engage in a meaningful conversation, make eye contact, and pick up on non-verbal cues. Spending too much time with electronic devices can also hinder the development of your communication skills. Just like how too much shade can stunt a plant's growth.

Mastering the art of effectively expressing your ideas, reading verbal and non-verbal cues, and responding appropriately to achieve your desired outcome are vital skills that grow more valuable as you get older. It's important to invest in honing your communication skills from a young age to set yourself up for success in your personal and professional life. *People with great communication skills can use their words to get the results that screams or fists can never achieve.*

When you graduate from high school, supervisors and professors will judge you and treat you based upon how well you can communicate. You'll be judged by every single adult from the time you enter a space until the time that you exit. **Poor communicators are not treated as well as good communicators** (ask Google). Employees who make $25 - $300 per hour (lots of jobs pay more than $70 per hour) have usually mastered the art of effectively communicating by the time they graduate from college or complete their training. Now is the time to practice by being an active participant in your classes. I'm hoping you don't want to join millions of adults who have embarrassingly limited communication skills. In that case, you need to have focused conversations with all kinds of people as often as possible.

Middle School to the Max!

High school is going to go by *so fast*. You won't believe me until it happens to you. If you decide to go to college, the military, or move to another state, you'll be exposed to hundreds of new topics, captivating experiences, and drastically different perspectives. You'll need all of your Spidey-senses (ask Google again) for these life-changing, mind-boggling moments. However, if your eyes are constantly glued to a screen or ears filled with buds, then your brain will be trained to be distracted. Sorry guys and gals, texting is not talking. Some social tools are popular because they're easy. I already covered how most rewards that come easy are lame.

Honestly, there are times when I'd love to wear my headphones or watch videos all day. People get on my nerves sometimes (tbh).

However, I exercise self-control and give every situation my undivided attention. I don't want *any* distractions to stop me from reaching more kids with my high school readiness tips. If your dreams are important to you too, then don't let a cellphone, lack of effort, bad attitude, or P.P. (see page 68) get in your way. Listen, you're not going to be a cute kid forever. It may not feel like it, but it's true. If you doubt me, please go look at your baby pictures. Time is going to keep passing. Ignoring the future isn't going to stop it from coming. Father Time is undefeated. True, some adults try to cling to their childhood. They're just being weird. Many are also being irresponsible. So, why not choose to put in the work right now to maximize your potential?

Middle School to the Max!

Reflecting on Your High School Readiness:

1) How are you when it comes to giving your teacher and classmates your undivided attention?

_____
_____
_____
_____

2) What do you need to do to detach from your cell phone and other distractions during school (you know yourself best, so dig deep and keep it real with yourself)?

_____
_____
_____
_____

3) What was your *aha* moment while reading about this topic?

_____
_____
_____
_____

Bridget K. Lambright

High School Readiness Task

At the end of every topic, this section is for you to write down 3-5 important ideas that your future high school self will need your middle school self to remember.

Middle School to the Max!

Be Steady

I understand that you might be ready for me to finish sharing these tips. I'm tired too. Was it surprising to learn how much goes into making the most of your middle school experience? If you didn't realize it before, that's okay. No one told me either. When I was younger, the adults in my life would often nag and yell. This caused me to tune them out. Unfortunately, I made a lot of spirit-crushing mistakes until I realized that I wasn't heading towards a happy future.

I'll keep this last tip brief. The Covid-19 pandemic has completely upended our world. Everyone's life has been impacted in some way. It's impossible to know who we would've been if the pandemic never happened. The virus has forced us to adapt and change. Some people have risen to the occasion and become the best version of themselves. Others have struggled and become the worst version of themselves. Remember I mentioned how fear is a powerful motivator?

I'm not the only one who's worried about you. Most adults are **freaking out** about all of the learning and growing time that you lost. We're looking at hundreds of missing hours that can never be redeemed. In other words, your brain is starving. Unlike your stomach, it's hard for you to hear the grumbling-rumbling. Lots of kids are being *extra* disruptive, defiant, or disrespectful in response to what they've lost. **Their pouting and angry outbursts are at an all-time high!** Is this you too?

Here's my final tip for you. Perhaps the most important one. Middle school is a crucial time to learn how to tune into your thoughts and feelings. It's essential to pay close attention to what's going on internally. Do you feel like there's sunshine, a cool breeze, fogginess, a storm, a flood, a heatwave, a hailstorm, or a tornado inside of you today? One way or another, your internal weather is going to influence your behaviors. When you aren't monitoring the weather, you risk being unprepared and unpredictable. Your inner person needs your attention now more than ever.

Middle school is a challenging time for teenagers. Your hormones are raging. Some friends may be drifting away. Your teachers are definitely

Middle School to the Max!

more demanding. Maybe your parents or guardians seem unbearable at times. Does it ever feel as though the life you used to know is changing at warp speed? Whether you feel like I've described you or not, please accept my virtual mama hug. Thousands of middle school students in buildings across America can't handle these changes. **Many are shutting down! Chaos is king!**

When you're at school, it's always a good idea to listen to yourself before responding to situations or people. There's a significant difference between reacting and responding. Emotions drive your reactions. Thinking drives your responses. Reacting can turn you into a problem-maker. It's **imperative** to learn to respond thoughtfully.

Strong emotions can be beneficial. Yet, it's essential to recognize when they're not serving you. When you listen to yourself, your inner person can be your friend. When you ignore your feelings, your inner person can become your enemy. You can feed your inner person by paying attention to your breathing, choosing your internal weather, and creating calming thoughts. Additionally, your school's guidance counselor can be a valuable resource for support.

Bridget K. Lambright

I understand that the world can be a stressful and an unfair place. I won't pretend that it gets much better as an adult. There's a lot of good and bad depending on the year, month, day, hour, minute, or second. However, I can promise you that by maximizing your middle and high school experiences (academically, emotionally, physically, and mentally), you'll be better equipped to face life's challenges. The most important relationship that you'll ever have in life is your relationship with yourself. I need you to pause. Read that relationship sentence again. Please try to save that nugget. The skills and knowledge you take upon *yourself* to gain everyday will serve you well in your future endeavors.

Remember, you deserve a future that makes you so blissfully happy that you feel like you're floating up in the clouds! You may already be happy now. But, I promise you, there are mind-blowing places to visit, outstanding people to meet, and extra special experiences out here in this big world that'll make you happier than you've ever been in your entire life. Yes, happier than getting spoiled on Christmas Day at Disney World. If you think that you've already seen all that this life has to offer, then I am here to tell you that you haven't even touched the tip of the tip of the

> Middle School to the Max!

tip of the tip of the iceberg yet. I have lived in five states and vacationed in several countries and three continents, but that's still nothing to brag about.

The earth is huge! Asia and Africa are the two largest continents even though they look small on a globe or map. You can go see as many states, countries, and continents as your precious heart desires. New places usually have new flavors that you've never tasted before. Never can be a good thing, but it can also be a sad thing. Here's why saying yes to your education matters so much. How do you want to live your next ten, twenty, thirty, forty, fifty, sixty, and seventy years? Celebrating or suffering? Only those willing to put in the work ever gain access to those highest levels of pure joy.

Bridget K. Lambright

Reflecting on Your High School Readiness:

1) Describe handling a stressful situation at school in a chaotic way versus in a controlled way.

___

2) When you feel as though there is a storm brewing inside of you, what do you need to **steady** yourself (you know yourself best, so dig deep and keep it real with yourself)?

___

3) What was your *aha* moment while reading about this topic?

___

Middle School to the Max!

High School Readiness Task

At the end of every topic, this section is for you to write down 3-5 important ideas that your future high school self will need your middle school self to remember.

Bridget K. Lambright

If you choose to put forth maximum effort, middle and high school won't feel pointless.

- **Ms. Lambright-Tommelleo**

Bonus Material:

Because I like *your* smile!

Bridget K. Lambright

My Life's Master Plan

My Mentality:

1) What is the purpose of middle school?

2) What is the purpose of high school?

3) How does your reason for coming to school compare to the purpose of middle school?

4) How much of you comes to school to get prepared to be successful in the future?

Circle One (1):

All of me

Most of me

Some of me

A little of me

None of me

5) Why would having a meaningful *Why* to come to school be important?

> Middle School to the Max!

6) What does your *Why* controls your *Try* mean?

My Life as an Adult:

7) I want my life's struggles to be -

   Circle one (1):

        Heartbreaking

        Hard

        Medium

        Smooth

        Easy

8) My House/Apartment Costs -

   Circle one (1):

        $500,000+

        $250,000+

        $100,000+

        $50,000+

        $15,000+

9) My Car Costs -

Circle one (1):

$50,000+

$25,000+

$10,000+

$5,000+

$1,000+

10) My State of Residence -

Circle one (1):

International

West Coast

East Coast

South

North

Midwest/Ohio

11) My Yearly Salary (pay) -

Circle one (1):

$500,000+

$250,000+

$100,000+

$50,000+

$15,000+

12) My Family -

Circle one (1):

Married with kids

Married

Single

13) My Dream Vacation Locations -

Circle all that apply:

Asia (China, Bali, Philippines, Dubai, India, etc.)

Africa (Nigeria, Kenya, Morocco, Ghana, Egypt, etc.)

North America (Canada, America, Mexico, Cuba, etc.)

South America (Brazil, Argentina, Peru, Columbia, etc.)

Antarctica

Europe (Italy, Germany, UK, Greece, France, Ireland, etc.)

Australia (New Zealand, Fiji, French Polynesia, etc.)

14) My Hobbies' Yearly Costs -

Circle one (1):

$50,000+

$25,000+

$10,000+

$5,000+

$1,000+

15) The Quality of My Healthcare (plus Dental & Vision) -

Circle one (1):

Excellent

Good

Fair

Poor

Terrible

None

16) My Education/Training -

Circle one (1):

Doctorate

Master's

Bachelor's/Certificate/Military

Associate

HS Diploma

None

17) My Savings Account -

Circle one (1):

$50,000+
$25,000+
$10,000+
$5,000+

Middle School to the Max!

$1,000+

$0

18) **My Retirement Savings (worked 30+ years) -**

Circle one (1):

$500,000+

$250,000+

$100,000+

$50,000+

$15,000+

$0

19) **My credit score for expensive purchases will be –**

(Circle one color)

20) When my family or close friends have a big emergency, I want to always have enough money to help the people who I love the most.

   Circle one (1):

   Absolutely

   Maybe

   No Way

21) What three (3) actions are you taking right *now* that are preparing you for your answers to questions 7 - 20?

Middle School to the Max!

In case you decide that middle school can help you with your *My Life's Master Plan*, here's how to get the most from the next few years:

1) Take a look at the 3-5 abilities that you listed after taking the *High School Readiness Survey* and rank them in the order that you want to work on them. Feel free to write your information on those pages. You can either start with the hardest ones or the easiest ones. Please don't try to work on all of them at the same time. Just tackle 1-2 at a time.

2) Reread my content for that topic(s) and measure how close you are to mastering those abilities. Create a short list of the behaviors and/or actions that you need to start doing or stop doing. Save this list in a place where you can easily see it.

3) Listen to advice. Believe in yourself. Remember your *Why* every single day.

4) Ask an adult and/or friend to be your Accountability Partner. He/She will help you keep track of your progress.

5) Practice. Correct. Practice. Correct. Practice. Correct. Practice...

Bridget K. Lambright

6) Retake that item on the survey.
7) Celebrate as your score(s) improve and move on to the next ability.
8) **You're a step closer to becoming a Maxstar (aka Rockstar)!**

Middle School to the Max!

High School Readiness Task

You made it to *The End*. Please write down 3-5 important ideas about *My Life's Master Plan* or a love/encouragement letter that your future high school self will need when faced with making THE big decision about staying committed to your education.

_____
_____
_____
_____
_____
_____
_____
_____
_____

www.ingramcontent.com/pod-product-compliance
Lightning Source LLC
Chambersburg PA
CBHW072052290426
44110CB00014B/1647